LIKE A KNOT IN MY SHOELACE

A *YAHRZEIT* REMEMBRANCE

by

Ilene Munetz Pachman

Illustrator: Karen Ostrove

SETH'S VERSION

ISBN:0-8381-0737-0

Dedicated to Steve and Scott's beloved and loving grandparents — Maurice, Jean, Leon and Alice — and in honor of their dear great-grandparents.

I.M.P.

Seth was painting a picture at the kitchen table. He dipped his paintbrush into yellow to paint a big sunshine. The paint set was a present from Grandpa Morris. He missed his grandpa. Seth painted a cloud. Grandpa Morris used to paint a lot, too, before he got so sick. Grandpa Morris died last year.

Seth watched the special candle glow inside the glass. His mother said it was called a *Yahrzeit* candle. She told Seth, "The candle will burn for 24 hours — all night and all day tomorrow. The flame will not go out until tomorrow night."

"We will light the *Yahrzeit* candle every year to help us remember Grandpa Morris," explained Seth's father.

"I already remember Grandpa Morris," thought Seth. He dipped his paintbrush into blue to paint the ocean. Seth remembered how his youthful grandpa had taught him how to float. He remembered how safe he had felt when Grandpa Morris tightly held his hand, as they jumped over the waves together. He thought about how his grandpa's wet beard had tickled his face when the older man bent down to give him a hug.

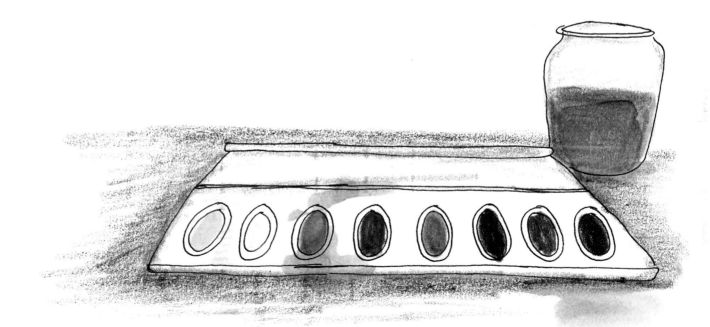

Seth remembered watching television with Grandpa Morris. He remembered how his grandpa would laugh hard at the funny parts on television. He remembered one time, when they were watching a sad movie together, Grandpa Morris even cried.

"I bet you didn't know men cried," his grandpa had said, wiping his eyes with a big handkerchief. "Well, they do. But most of the time, you can't see it, because their tears stay in their hearts. But those tears are real, too."

Seth dipped his paintbrush into red. He painted a big heart and a little heart next to the cloud. He looked at the *Yahrzeit* candle. "I guess it works," Seth thought, remembering more things about his grandpa.

He remembered how much Grandpa Morris had enjoyed planting flowers and trimming the bushes. Seth's mother used to say, "Taking care of the garden, the way your grandpa does, is a *mitzvah*. It's something God wants us to do."

Seth dipped his paintbrush into green to paint a tree. Seth remembered how Grandpa Morris could always get the knots out of his shoelaces — even better than Seth's father could — even the double knots.

He remembered how his grandpa had taught him and his brother how to play cards, like Casino and Contest. Seth knew that Contest was really a card game called War. But his grandpa didn't like the name War. His grandpa liked peace.

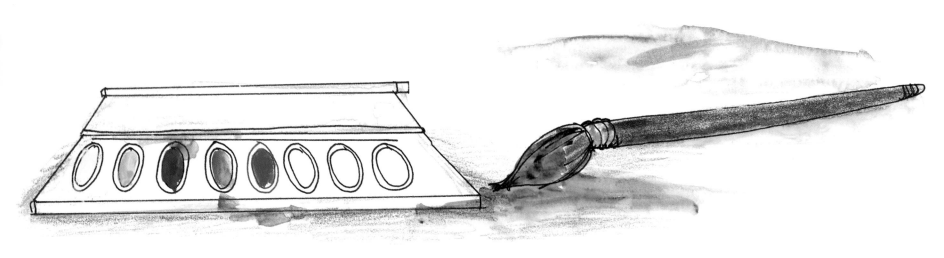

Seth dipped the paintbrush again and again, until he made a rainbow. Then he painted a dove, a dove of peace, like on the front of the synagogue.

Seth remembered that after Grandpa Morris' funeral, people said, "May he rest in peace."

Seth remembered how, at the funeral, many people cried, even grown men and women. His mother cried. His father cried more. His brother cried the most. Seth remembered, "I didn't cry. It was like a knot in my shoelace."

Then, he remembered again what Grandpa Morris had said about the tears we don't see. "Those tears are real, too."

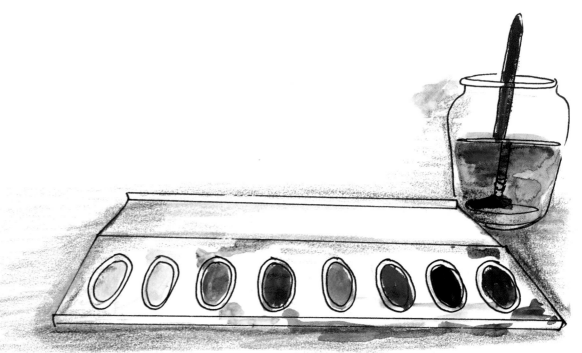

Seth painted a teardrop inside the small heart. He remembered there were times, during the year, when tears for Grandpa Morris did roll down his cheeks. He painted raindrops under the cloud. He painted more raindrops, to water the tree in his picture.

Seth thought again about the fun times he and his grandpa had shared.

Now, Seth's father often said, "Grandpa Morris made us feel happy because he truly enjoyed life. To enjoy life, like Grandpa Morris did, is a *mitzvah*."

Seth dipped his paintbrush back into the yellow paint to make the rainbow bigger. While the *Yahrzeit* candle continued to glow, Seth painted words of love across the rainbow: "For Grandpa Morris. I'll never forget you."

Beth painted a teardrop inside the small heart. She remembered there were times, during the year, when tears for Grandpa Morris did roll down her cheeks. She painted raindrops under the cloud. She painted more raindrops, to water the tree in her picture.

Beth thought again about the fun times she and her grandpa had shared.

Now, Beth's father often said, "Grandpa Morris made us feel happy because he truly enjoyed life. To enjoy life, like Grandpa Morris did, is a *mitzvah*."

Beth dipped her paintbrush back into the yellow paint to make the rainbow bigger. While the *Yahrzeit* candle continued to glow, Beth painted words of love across the rainbow: "For Grandpa Morris. I'll never forget you."

Beth dipped the paintbrush again and again, until she made a rainbow. Then she painted a dove, a dove of peace, like on the front of the synagogue.

Beth remembered that after Grandpa Morris' funeral, people said, "May he rest in peace."

Beth remembered how, at the funeral, many people cried, even grown men and women. Her mother cried. Her father cried more. Her brother cried the most. Beth remembered, "I didn't cry. It was like a knot in my shoelace."

Then, she remembered again what Grandpa Morris had said about the tears we don't see. "Those tears are real, too."

Beth dipped her paintbrush into green to paint a tree. Beth remembered how Grandpa Morris could always get the knots out of her shoelaces — even better than Beth's father could — even the double knots.

She remembered how her grandpa had taught her and her brother how to play cards, like Casino and Contest. Beth knew that Contest was really a card game called War. But her grandpa didn't like the name War. Her grandpa liked peace.

Beth dipped her paintbrush into red. She painted a big heart and a little heart next to the cloud. She looked at the *Yahrzeit* candle. "I guess it works," Beth thought, remembering more things about her grandpa.

She remembered how much Grandpa Morris had enjoyed planting flowers and trimming the bushes. Beth's mother used to say, "Taking care of the garden, the way your grandpa does, is a *mitzvah*. It's something God wants us to do."

Beth remembered watching television with Grandpa Morris. She remembered how her grandpa would laugh hard at the funny parts on television. She remembered one time, when they were watching a sad movie together, Grandpa Morris even cried.

"I bet you didn't know men cried," her grandpa had said, wiping his eyes with a big handkerchief. "Well, they do. But most of the time, you can't see it, because their tears stay in their hearts. But those tears are real, too."

"I already remember Grandpa Morris," thought Beth. She dipped her paintbrush into blue to paint the ocean. Beth remembered how her youthful grandpa had taught her how to float. She remembered how safe she had felt when Grandpa Morris tightly held her hand, as they jumped over the waves together. She thought about how her grandpa's wet beard had tickled her face when the older man bent down to give her a hug.

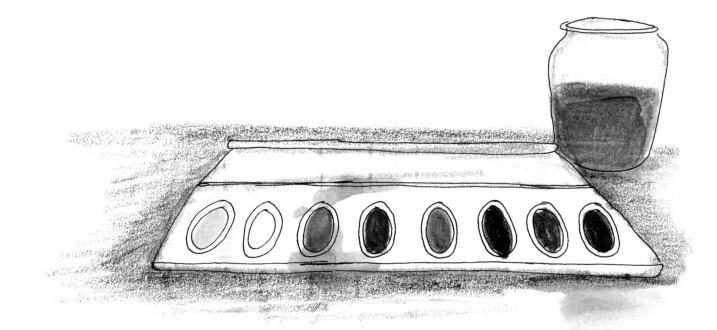

Beth watched the special candle glow inside the glass. Her mother said it was called a *Yahrzeit* candle. She told Beth, "The candle will burn for 24 hours — all night and all day tomorrow. The flame will not go out until tomorrow night."

"We will light the *Yahrzeit* candle every year to help us remember Grandpa Morris," explained Beth's father.

Beth was painting a picture at the kitchen table. She dipped her paintbrush into yellow to paint a big sunshine. The paint set was a present from Grandpa Morris. She missed her grandpa. Beth painted a cloud. Grandpa Morris used to paint a lot, too, before he got so sick. Grandpa Morris died last year.

ISBN:0-8381-0737-0

*Dedicated to Steve and Scott's beloved and loving
grandparents — Maurice, Jean, Leon and Alice —
and in honor of their dear great-grandparents.*

I.M.P.

LIKE A KNOT IN MY SHOELACE

A *YAHRZEIT* REMEMBRANCE

by

Ilene Munetz Pachman

Illustrator: Karen Ostrove

BETH'S VERSION